RAITONG

THE INNOCENT IN ASHES

EDITED BY EHBOKLANG PYNGROPE

Made with ♥ on the Notion Press Platform
www.notionpress.com

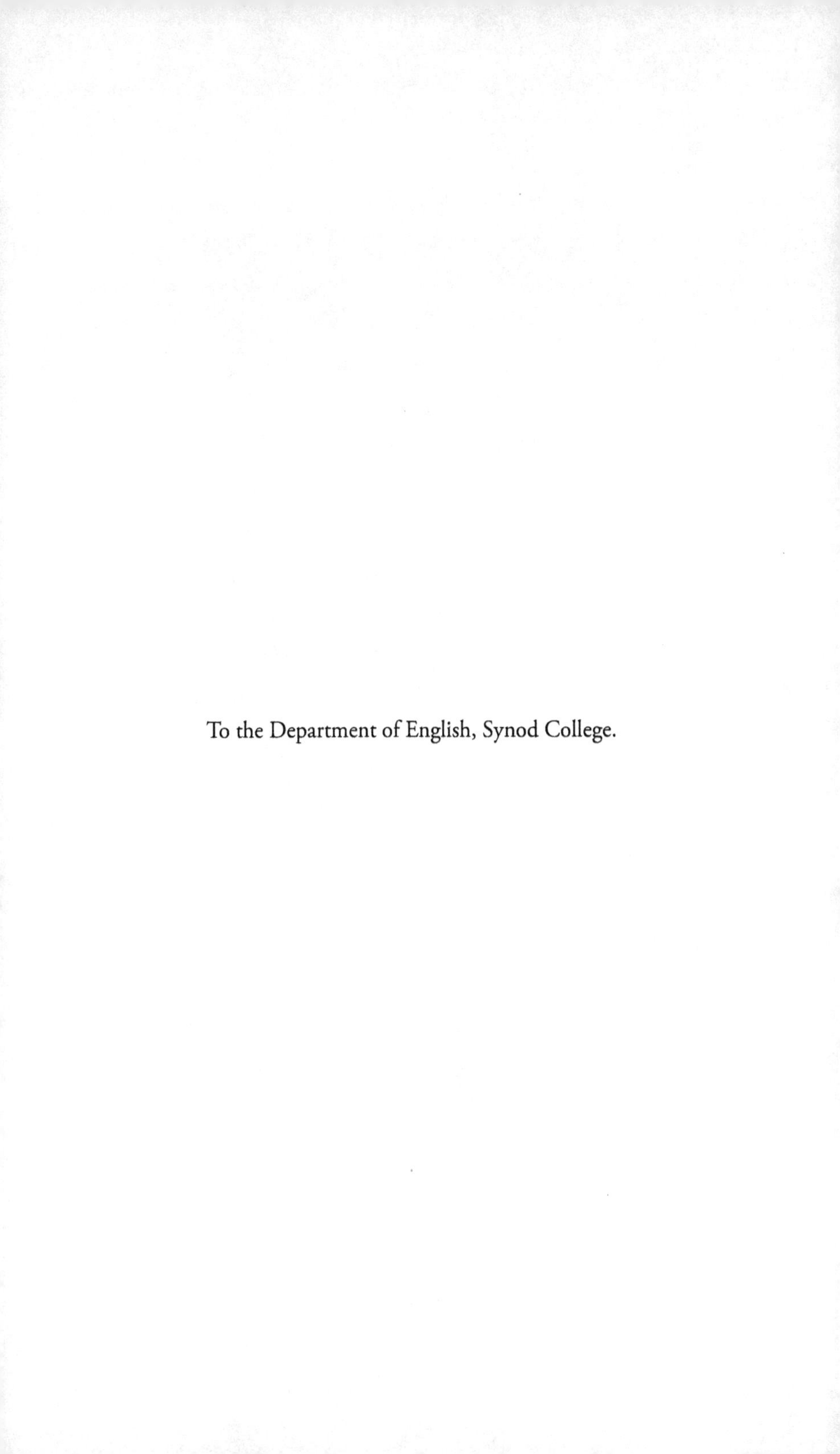

To the Department of English, Synod College.

Contents

Foreword — vii

Preface — ix

Acknowledgements — xiii

Prologue — xv

1. Persara L. — 1

2. Badakynti N. I. — 3

3. Mewanpynbiang N. — 5

4. Ophelia L. — 7

5. Ladianghunshisha S. — 9

6. Damon J. — 11

7. Niwan M. — 13

8. Jeocyqueen W. — 15

9. Plieladkyrhai R. — 18

10. Saphidahun K. — 21

11. Ibadahun L. M. — 22

12. Maphibanlum K. — 24

13. Kelly L. S. — 26

14. Mewanraplang K. — 28

15. Meba-ai-habanbiang L. — 30

16. Mebalarishisha N. — 32

17. Mattibakor M. — 34

18. Skhemborlang K. — 36

19. Henry V. M. — 37

20. Erica N. M. — 40

21. Evangelyne S. — 42

22. Jankincy H. L. — 45

Contents

23. Ehboklang P.   47

24. Glossary   48

Foreword

There are stories that live beyond time, imprinted into our cultural memories, whispered through generations, and kept alive through signs and mnemonics. *Raitong* is one such story—an echo of love, longing, defiance, and loss that continues to haunt the Khasi hills. The poems in this anthology reimagines age-old tragedy, capturing its sorrow and beauty with voices as distinct as they are poignant.

Through these verses, Love, desires and death rise again, carried on the wind, mourned in the fire. Manik's music, his passion, and his ill-fated love for the Queen Lieng Makaw testify to the current of death that propels each desire as if every longing heart is one more step toward obliterating one's own self. Each poem here is also a rekindling of that flame—a meditation on love both sacred and forbidden, on the cost of desire, and on the resilience of memory.

The poets gathered in this collection have engaged with the legend in their own ways—some through the eyes of Manik himself, others through the voice of the Queen, the baby and even that of the *besli* itself. Yet, what unites them all is the weight of fate and the struggle between love and power, duty and freedom.

This anthology does not merely retell a story—it resurrects its soul. In these lines, fire burns again, melodies echo once more, and we are reminded that passion, no matter how tragic its end, leaves a mark that cannot be erased.

To those who listen closely, the flute still plays.

Lede E-Miki Pohshna (Ph.D, MCS)

Preface

Raitong, *The Innocent in Ashes*, is an anthology produced by the students and teachers of the Department of English, Synod College, Shillong. It is another attempt to create spaces and narratives of an old age Khasi folktale, and this anthology focused on *U Manik Raitong*. It is also an attempt to initiate an on-going reflection and rendition of various Khasi Myths, Legends and Folktales through poetry, presenting buried perspectives, following the first anthology, *Likai*.

The book is an accumulation of 23 poems, each with its own perception on Manik Raitong and his woeful tale. We had every bit of pleasure and joy writing these poems and we wish you have a pleasant read as we take you on our journey of Raitong, *The Innocent in Ashes*.

The Poets of Synod College.

The Poets of Synod College, Department of English.

Dr. Persara Lyngdoh, Assistant Professor.

Dr. Badakynti N. Iangngap, Assistant Professor.

Mewanpynbiang Nongkhlaw, II Semester, English Major.

Ophelia Lyndem, II Semester, English Major.

Ladianghunshisha Sohliya, II Semester, English Major.

Damon Jyrwa, II Semester, English Major.

Niwan Mawlong, IV Semester, English Major.

Jeocyqueen War, IV Semester, English Major.

Plieladkyrhai Ryntathiang, IV Semester, English Major.

Saphidahun Kharnaior, VI Semster, English Honours.

Ibadahun L. Marshillong, VI Semster, English Honours.

Maphibanlum Kurkalang, VI Semster, English Honours.

Kelly Lona Syiem, VI Semster, English Honours.

Mewanraplang Kharbuli, VI Semster, English Honours.

Meba-ai-habanbiang Lyndem, VI Semster, English Honours.

Mebalarishisha Nongsiej, VI Semster, English Honours.

Mattibakor Marbaniang, VI Semster, English Honours.

Skhemborlang Kharshiing, VI Semster, English Honours.

Henry V. Marboh, VI Semster, English Honours.

Erica N. Myrthong, VI Semster, English Honours.

Evangelyne Shabong, VI Semester, English Honours.

Jankincy H. Lyngdoh, Guest Lecturer.

Dr. Ehboklang Pyngrope, Assistant Professor.

Acknowledgements

We owe our deepest sense of gratitude to Dr. G. Lyngdoh, Principal, Synod College, Shillong, Dr. M. Rani, Vice- Principal, Synod College, Shillong and Dr. W. Kharmawphlang, IQAC coordinator, Synod College, Shillong for their unwavering support in all our endeavours.

A bouquet of thanks to Smt. I. Pyngrope, Head, Department of English, for motivating us in all our attempts and intentions, providing valuable insights to our undertakings. We owe our heartfelt appreciation to the teachers of the English Department, Synod College, for their continuous support and encouragement.

We owe a debt of gratitude to our family and friends who constantly encourages us to do the very best and whose belief in us has been instrumental in our success.

Above all else, we owe our gratitude to God, for his perpetual kindness and unwavering blessings.

Thanking you.

The Poets of Synod College.

Dr. E. Pyngrope,
Editor,
Raitong.

Prologue

Manik Raitong is an ancient Khasi folktale. Manik was an orphan who lost his parents at an early age and there was no one to take care of him. Being left all alone, people would call him a *raitong* or a pitiful and helpless person. Throughout his life, he would always mourn and his heart was full of sorrows. In order to distract himself, he made a *Besli*, which is a flute made from bamboo tree. He would play it beautifully all throughout the night till morning comes. Then, one night, Lieng Makaw, the King's wife, heard him play and wondered who the person was. Afterwards, she saw Manik with his *Besli*, and started to persuade him to commit adultery. He rebelled against her but eventually he fell into her trap. Then, the Queen was pregnant and bore a boy child. After a few months, the King arrived and felt disheartened by this incident. For justice to prevail, he asked every man to bring one banana and to whom where this child goes, would be its father. Then, Manik came and at this point, this child immediately exalted at his arrival. The King understood everything, and asked Manik to be eliminated. Manik pleaded that he would want to be burnt alive. At this point, he felt hopeless and despaired. He marched backwards to the summit while playing a sad lyrical tone. He walked round the flame three times, subsequently he struck his *Besli* upside-down into the ground and went into the burning flames. Along this time, the Queen also jumped into the fire with her lover. Afterwards, all that was left were ashes and only came out an upside down *shken* which is a preferred type of bamboo that is use for flute making. This burning place is still prevalent till date. This story is legendary and is famously retold among the Khasi tribes.

Kelly L. S.

1. Persara L.

It is said that

Fire burns

Fire purges

Fire devours everything in its path.

Then why did the ashes

Generate new life?

Bamboos, green and vibrant

Though upside down.

Did the fire distort them?

Even so, they are alive and thriving

Living relics of a passion.

A passion so intense

It transgresses boundaries

Of class, of gender, of pretence.

A passion for love:

It lives in the tiny bundle of joy

Or is it a bundle of wrath

Waiting to avenge

The circumstances of its existence?

A passion for music

That breathes beauty

Wherever it's heard.

Its sublimity

Alters dynamics of desire

And politics of power.

It shatters barriers
Of convictions,
Of intentions,
It instigates actions.

2

The cresendo is reached.
The fire burns.
The music stops.

But not before
It had tug and kindle
The embers of longing,
Of memory and storytelling,
Of communion
Among all
Other "*raitongs*".

2. Badakynti N. I.

He is your Orpheus
With his flute.
Poems written,
Songs composed,
For the wretched of our earth-
Your *raitong*.
Purged by the fire,
An avatar celebrated.

Yet I was there.
I saw him first,
Knew him first,
Loved him first,
Celebrated him first.
I do not deserve
Your adulations and adorations
I cooked him in that fire.

What could a privileged princess want from the wretched?

His music hugged
The crevices of my heart
Like smoke
Its smell lingered
Till I wanting more

Crept in the night-
Like smoke
To the lap of his hearth.

I wasn't miserable,
I had it all.
More wretched is the wretched.
I lit the pyre.
Spurn me all you like,
Yet I am also wretched,
Kordit.
Woe is she who dared
To fall in love,
Yet I was also loved,
Loved too much.
But I am not a Helen
I am Lieng Makaw.

3. Mewanpynbiang N.

Upon the whispering hills of Meghalaya,
Where echoes roam,
Live Manik with kin, his heart their home.
But Fate, unkind, in shadows crept,
And tore from him the love he kept.
By Heaven's will, his dearest gone,
A lonesome soul, now left alone.

The hills stood still, the river sight,
As Manik played and softly cried.
His flute sang tales of love and woe;
Of hearts that burned, but could not glow.

Lieng Makaw, her soul entranced,
By notes that made the moonlight dance.
She longed to break her gilded chains;
To chase the lay through mist and rains.
She heard his tune, so wild, so free,
A song that called her heart to flee.
They met in love, but love denied.

As fate had been cruel, so too was love unkind,
A tale so sweet, yet sorrow entwined.
For She a Belle, with dignity crowned,
A jewel in chains, in silence bound.

Behind the veil of royal guise,
A caged soul with weary eyes.

The wrathful king with heart of steel,
Declared their love a crime to feel.
And so, would shatter hearts, would clip off his wings,
With chains and ruthless might, he took off everything;
Cast Manik to flames untold.

Yet still, his song was brave and bold,
A melody fierce, a tale retold.
As the fire took his breath,
His music lived beyond his death.

4. Ophelia L.

Our worlds defined, our souls met and reconciled
My simple flute brought you to me,
Its soft and sweet melody,
And our secret meetings, softly flew.
Time and Space the worlds judgement weighs
Like iron rules, fleeting moments, cold and cruel.

Our story yet untold, for you, a lineage proud and old.
For all we ever wished was a world of what might be
Yet they built walls so strong and high
And therefore, our broken vows here shall lie.

They casted a flame of shame so bright of crimson haze.
I walked into the burning flames, unfazed.
A sacrifice so grand, where crackling tongues on all sides,
Where the world was then a canvas painted in shades of grey.
Yet I feel no pain,nor fear, nor shadows could deter
For all I could ever think of was Her.

My doubts dissolved; my fears casted aside
As I walk into those flames that night
And our Love's pure essence abides.
For the flame of shame was meant to break two souls,
Stead formed an unbreakable bond, where hope resides,
For a happy ever after, or what could have been

But as for now the world consider this a Sin.

But therefore still, our broken Hearts shall forever bore

A legacy, A tragic love story

A love denied that could not last

For my shattered heart is in silence still,

As we part ways in a tragic dance, a silent plea.

For what our souls were meant to be

For our tragic tale, our love denied.

A Mournful chime for their captive minds.

5. Ladianghunshisha S.

An archetypal tragic love this was,
Born in longing, bound in silence,
A flickering fire never meant to last.

I loved her in stolen moments,
Where words were scarce but eyes confessed.
In the hush of dawn, in the hush of dusk,
We were everything and nothing at once.
But love, no matter how softly held,
Leaves echoes too loud to hide.
And so, hands tore us apart,
Voices turned our love to sin.

She remained, adorned in gold,
A queen untouched, a prisoner still.
And I, stripped of even the right to grieve,
Became a man without a home.

But love does not fade—it burns.
And so, I stepped into the fire,
Where the warmth felt like her touch,
Where the flames knew my name.

Now, I am nothing but smoke in the wind,
A whisper in the trees, a song in the river.

But love—love is never silent.
It lingers, even in ashes.

An archetypal tragic love this was,
And love like this never dies.

6. Damon J.

Beneath the sky so vast and so wide,
I walk alone with fate as my guide.
This heart once filled with love so true,
Now bathed in this sorrow's endless hue

Fair woman, light of mine,
Bound to another by fates design.
Yet still in my soul, your name is sung,
A melody, yet left unsung.

This world has turned it's gazes so cold,
Their whispers sharp, their judgements so bold.
My love, they scorn, they call it shame,
Yet love like mine, knows no blame.

They took you far, they cast me low,
A wounded heart with pain to sow.
Yet in my hands- my flue remains,
A song of grief- this song of chains.

So, hear me now! Silent night!
I pray for love; I pray for right.
Let this time, I'm sorrow steep,
A tale of love that none shall keep.

And when the flames embrace me whole,
Let smoke and song rise from my soul.
For though my body turns to dust,
My love shall live- it shall now rust.

7. Niwan M.

In a small village under a quiet sky,
Manik, an orphan, could only ask why.
No warm embrace, no gentle care,
Just his flute to hold his despair.

With each breath, his flute would cry,
A lonely sound beneath the sky.
No song escaped his lips, only the weeping flute,
A melody of sorrow, fragile yet absolute.

But one dark day, the king's wife drew near,
Drawn by the echoes of his tune so clear.
She forced her touch upon his heart,
A vile act that tore him apart.

Manik did no wrong, yet bore the blame,
Punished for a crime he never claimed.
The village judged with blinded cries,
Their anger rising to darkened skies.

They lit a fire to end his pain,
Condemning an innocent, lost in flame.
Now his echoes linger in the mourning breeze,
A sorrowful tale that never leaves.

His flute spoke where words could not,
A voice of grief the world forgot.
Manik, the lonely boy, lost to fire,
A pure heart silenced, turned to ashes.

8. Jeocyqueen W.

Among the wilderness,
I heard a melancholic melody;
Echoes of a mournful song
Carried out by the besli,
Wondering what drove him
To pour his grief into haunting harmonies;
That even I, I sank deeply;
Darkness and silence seem to be his only companions,
On his small hut where he's abandoned;
His hidden depths summons me to explore
The whisper in mine, grows to a resolute call;
I was swept away by the depth of his eyes,
I'm on a spell unaware of my own demise;
In the shadows of wrong,
My heart betrays all reason;
T'was a forbidden beacon.

My heart was whole with moon
That shone so bright,
A flame between us that would never die;
He's like a seed carried by the air,
His mind drift away with dark despair.
The winds of fortune blew us
In a different direction,
Yet my heart aflutter beats for him alone;

Fate beckoned him away,
To a world beyond our sea
Our love's a lingering shadow, a reminder
Of what will never be;
With sleepless nights, my heart foreboding mist settles,
Shrouded my soul,
As I tremble at the thought of losing him,
Fears me the worst;
My tears a bitter rain fall for the ruin I've wrought,
For in his eyes a light once shone,
Now dimmed by my hand and thoughts.

A bitter harvest I reap,
This is my biggest regret,
Led Manik, a kind soul to this dark pit I created;
The shadow of mortality looms over him,
I'm powerless to save him,
My dying dream.
While the hunger and raging fire devours his soul,
This pain I felt can never be told;
In a million shards of sorrow my heart lie,
This thorn that pricks,
Urge me to die;
With every beat,
My heart whispered "With him, I die",
While leaving my man's seed with my king;
In the realm of unknown,
May our love take root,
Let us meet again my beacon of hope.

Love's alchemy transforms the ordinary
Like *U Shken* thriving upside down in history.

• 17 •

9. Plieladkyrhai R.

They built me high, they fed me well,
With timber strong and flames from hell.
A sentence passed, a fate was sealed,
A love too bold, a wound unhealed.

But long before my embers glowed,
Before the trial, before the woe,
A melody upon the air
Had called a Queen, so young, so fair.

"Ka 'per amirphor jingieid,
Ha thmied-kpep ding,
U Manik bad Lieng ki shad iphuh - iphieng."

His flute had sung, the wind had swayed,
And through the night, she found her way.
A wretched man, a cursed soul,
Yet in his tune, she felt him whole.

The stolen nights, the whispered sighs,
A love that bloomed beneath the skies.
But love in secret, love in shame,
Would soon be swallowed by my flame.

The crowd stood still, their hearts unsure,

For never had they seen before
A man so cursed, a man so torn,
Yet standing proud, yet so adorned.

His fingers danced, the music wept,
A tune so deep, the heavens slept.
And as he played, she broke the chains,
A Queen defying law's remains.

She ran to him, she took his hand,
Before the flames, they made their stand.

The King, the crowd, in silent dread,
Watched love rise high, where fear had fled.
She cast her crown, she shed her name,
And leaped with him into my flame.

I swallowed them, I burned, I roared,
Yet in my depths, their love still soared.
No cries, no screams, just warmth, just light,
Two souls entwined in endless flight.

And as they fell, as fire sighed,
A whispered vow, their love still cried—

"Ka jingim, Manik bad Lieng ki ieid shitrhem,
Poh ka Lawarding, ki kdup ki piam shilem."

I was meant to end, to take, to break,

Yet all I did was bend, remake.
For love like this, so fierce, so bright,
Can never burn, but only ignite.

Now in the hills, in winds that wail,
Their song still floats, it tells the tale.
And I, the pyre, once meant to part,
Have only joined two fearless hearts.

10. Saphidahun K.

Oh! Sorrow song sung by the flute
Echo by the hills heard the ones who have ears
Felt by my lover,
Wrapped with clay and let the world shall not see me
Where I found more of myself, less of the world
Night by Night the song of love carried by the wind
Whispers and calling my lover drawn to her heart
Time has spared me, yet what remains?
A heart that beats in silence and none
All I did was to love, no sword no sin
I raised nor did, but what remains?
Fate left me alone again with cruel hands
Had I not hidden my love for her
Perhaps would have to live the night
All I did was to give love, love gave me death
Will my lover shed her tears?
Will my flute cries in pain?
Will my song be heard by the ears again?
But I fell and my love remains.

11. Ibadahun L. M.

I was born out of sin and nobody knew my name
A story untold, A truth concealed
In the shadows I live without love and care
Mother's shame that kept me secret and left me to bear

"Who is the father?" they whispered
A questions that haunted without a care
A secret kept a truth concealed
A father's identity unrevealed

It was an ordinary man who betrayed the king
Stolen by his goddess and left a love unknown
She draped in sorrowed white
She followed him into the night.

I watched them both consumed by flame
The only love I'd ever claim
I did not cry, I did not scream
For all I lost was just a dream

A hidden truth cannot be kept for long
The parents death as the king discovers
Oh how I long to be held in love and care
I'd rather not exist than experiencing their lost

A father's death, a protector lost
A Goddess betrayal a kingdom cost
A test was made, a fate was sealed
Truth uncovered, no lies concealed.

12. Maphibanlum K.

In Khasi hills, where legends reside,
A tale of Manik Raitong, with love as his guide.
Orphaned and lone, with a heart full of song,
He turned to music, where he truly belonged.
In Ri-Bhoi's heart, a melody began,
Manik, the wretched, a soulful young man.

He met a fair sovereign so bright,
Ka Lieng Makaw, bathed in love's light.
But fate, it seems, had a cruel design,
For Lieng was betrothed, her heart not her own,
The *Syiem* awaited, but her love remained true,
To Manik Raitong, and the songs they once knew.

In secret they met, beneath the starlit sky,
Their love blossomed, as time hurried by.
A child was born, a love's tender sign,
But shadows loomed, as the truth did unwind.
Accused and condemned, for love's sweet embrace,
Manik was sentenced, to a tragic disgrace.

Yet given a choice, of how life would end,
He chose a pyre, where love would transcend.
Dressed in finery, with flute in his hand,
He played a last song, across the Khasi land.

Then leapt into flames, with a heart full of woe,
Lieng followed swiftly, where true love must go.
From ashes arose, a spring pure and clear,
Bamboos sprouted high, banishing all fear.
A tree with boat-shaped leaves, a symbol so grand,
Lieng Makaw's memory, forever in this land.

So, listen closely, to the whispers of the breeze,
For in every note, Manik's spirit appeases.
A tale of true love, both tragic and deep,
Manik Raitong's legend, forever we'll keep.

13. Kelly L. S.

A "*Raitong*", they call me
A name, I do not plea
I want to resist this identity
For I fear, it will forever be my misery.

I crafted my fate,
Through the holes I penetrate.
That let out a mourning sound
That accompanies me on the ground.

In black nights, I amuse
A sound, in lyrical tune.
Stranger afar, had a fond
Unaware, I will bond.
A royal hand, I refuse to win
That would lead me to sin.

Those forbidden hands, clutched like a trap,
I cannot combat.
Her imperial body, so tempting
Too weak, I lost in rebelling.
A disgrace, displayed
A son, left a strayed.

I have fallen from grace.

And therefore, penalty is in place
As I seek forward
It is only death to entertain,
Which again I cannot refrain.

A "*Raitong*" I am, I admit
As I travelled backwards to the summit.
People gathered to see,
As I paved the way to be
Among the flames that awaited me.

14. Mewanraplang K.

Why has my life turned out this way,

Trapped in an abyss where shadows sway?

All I seek is love, a hand to hold,

But the world feels distant, bitter, and cold.

No warmth, no comfort, just an aching heart,

The king and I remain worlds apart.

But through the pain, the melody so sweet,

A healing song that makes me complete.

I wonder where this sound is from,

A tune that makes my heart beat strong.

I searched the kingdom, lost in the sound,

Until I found him, love unbound.

Manik Raitong with his *besli* a soul so pure,

His love brought peace, a perfect cure.

The king returned, his wrath untold,

He heard the news, his heart turned cold.

He called for a ring of fire so bright,

And forced Manik to face the night.

I watched in pain, my heart in tears,

As love was crushed by all my fears.

But in that moment, love's fire burned,

I leapt with him, no matter the turn.

Oh, poor Manik, what have I done?

Why must you suffer for love we've won?

If only fate had been kinder, we'd be free,

But now we burn together, just him and me.

15. Meba-ai-habanbiang L.

Life is cruel to me, I'm full of grief,
Death stole my parents; like a thief.
They say time will be kind, time will heal,
But the gloom and sorrow is all I feel.
Clothe in ash, I look for solace,
To survive, and not become a menace.
Condolences I received from fellow men,
Did not ease me, though I pretend.
I need some higher power to get me going,
Something divine, something empowering.
So I pick up my flute in desperation,
To fill the emptiness and isolation.
I play like my life depends on the tune, I play before bed,
I play like I wanted to survive, like I'm hanging on a single thread,
I continued to form a cry for comfort, with majors and minors,
Not aware of who listens and who remembers,
The melodies, and the sound of loneliness,
But I was wrong, because I was met with a test.
She heard my flute, she heard the sound,
She said "Your melodies, a treasure found",
She pled, she stayed to hear me play,
I was deceived; I could not send her away.
Weak and confused I fell, trapped in her net,
Now the consequences I'll face because of it.
Now tell me if my music is deceitful?

If only I knew then, I'd be more careful,

I searched for peace, I found death,

The irony of life, I wish I never met.

People now only talk in sympathy,

They shook their heads, they mourn for me,

"Oh Manik!", they said, "Your melodies were overwhelmingly beautiful,

But your melodies burnt you to ashes, how pitiful!

I wish life would have been kinder to you, but life turned to dust,

It seems Life has been harsh and cruel to all of us!"

16. Mebalarishisha N.

Your voice echoed, and my heart stood still,
I'm addicted to it; I'll never have my fill.
I see you in my dreams, even when I'm awake
I'll wait for you, no matter how long it will take.

The tune of your *besli* makes me want to tarry.
I'm undone—this is beyond the ordinary.
What is magic, if not the spell you've casted upon me?
Oh, So powerful! –this strong hold you have on me.

Though turmoil rages deep within my soul,
If I pursue you, will you be able to make me whole?
Should I follow my heart, or head morality?
This forbidden love or my royalty?

But I have chosen, and I'm waiting for you to obey.
This love I bear for you makes me willing my husband to betray.
Don't you see, I've long for this day,
They call it sin—I call it fate.

I'm in love with you, though bound by vows,
Yet I cannot stop—my heart is yours now.
This love so wrong yet it feels so right,
Lie with me, Manik, hold me tight.

Honor and royalty now mean nothing to me,
No crown or jewel could change what I see.
They gave me riches, but you gave me purpose,
and our child, our world—our love's purest surface.

I do not know where our future may lead,
The king will know of our secret misdeeds.
But come what may, I will stand by your side,
For I have chosen you as my love and my life.

17. Mattibakor M.

Being married to a king, and while he's away
The many responsibilities to meet;
To put all things in places
For the kingdom not to fall apart.

After a long day, I lay tired in bed
My body ache, silently moan
I long for my husband's hands
To drive the weariness away.

My eyes halfway closed,
As the blanket about to get weirdly comfortable
A melody struck my ears,
It echoes nearer and nearer as I rush towards it.

From my balcony, I noticed
A man sat with his *besli* tune
The freezing night tortures me
But all I can feel is a soothing embrace.

Almost every night, yearning for the melody,
Every tune, a relaxing emotion it derives
Every note, sends a relief to my soul
I've got sleepless nights but my heart is content.

"Is this what I'm searching for?"
"Is it suitable for me? "
"Am I allowed to peek? "
"Am I allowed to love you?"

Being a silent audience is quite tiresome
But I'd like to keep things that way
Keep reminding myself and say
"Maybe in another life."

18. Skhemborlang K.

In a small hut lived a young man
Called Manik Raitong
A man pure in heart and soul.
He lived all alone. In a world of hatred
Blame Raitong for dead curse.

Living in, disheartened environment
Judging him.
With the eyes of an eagle,
And their thoughts of dislikes
That stress upon him.

Manik found love, but ended in sorrow
Music and tune, his only companion
Lighter to feel, he played.

Oh! how sad to see him, dying.

In a circle of suffocating hope,
Neither love was meant for him
Now was it given to him.
And hatred, became his choice.

19. Henry V. M.

There was once a man who held me close,
His hands worn, cracked by time,
But when he touched me, he was light as breath,
As if the weight of the world
Could be lifted in a single note.

He carved me from silence,
Shaped me from a quiet tree,
And in my hollow, he found his voice.
Through me, he spoke in sorrow,
In longing, in love
That had nowhere else to go.

By night, he played
Low, aching, unbroken.
The melody curled into the dark,
Soft enough to be a secret,
Loud enough to be a prayer.

Then she came, wrapped in silk and moonlight,
Her eyes deep wells of wanting.
She did not love the man,
Only the way his fingers danced,
Only the way his song filled empty spaces
She could not bear to sit in.

She reached for him,
Pleaded, promised, whispered sin.
But his music was not for her.
He played for the wind, for the stars,
For the ache inside his chest.

And so, love turned bitter.
So, the world turned cruel.
They came with ropes, with rage,
Ripped him from my voice,
Dragged him toward the fire's hungry breath.

Still, he held me, still he played.
A song for truth, for loss, for fate
A song that could not be undone.

Three times he turned, slow as dawn,
And placed me in the waiting earth.
Then he stepped forward, unafraid,
Into the burning light.

She followed, whether out of love or ruin,
I do not know.

The fire took them both.
The night wept.
The music stilled.

Now I wait beneath the soil,
My voice quiet but unbroken.
The world forgets, the wind moves on,
But I remember.

• 39 •

Still, I mourn.
Still, I play.

20. Erica N. M.

A love so true, a heart so blind,
I gave my all, my heart and mind.
But little did I know, a deceitful snare
Lurked in the shadows, a love that wasn't there.

Her heart was stolen by a melody sweet,
Manik's songs, a siren's call, her soul to greet.
She fell under his spell, a love so strong and free,
Torn between two hearts, a choice she couldn't see.

I searched for answers, night and day,
For the father of the child, in a secret way.
But when the truth revealed, my heart turned to stone,
I burned with anger, my love, now overthrown.

I thought our love was pure and true,
Now I'm left with just a memory or two,
Of laughter, tears, and whispers in the night,
A bittersweet reminder of love that lost its light.

The flames that consumed them, a fiery, fatal sleep,
My heart, a heavy burden, my soul, a deep creep.
I weep not for their love, but for mine, now lost,
A king's justice, a heart's unforgiving cost.

In the ashes, I see my heart's remains,
A love, a trust, a bond, all reduced to flames.
I am the king, the law, the judge, the fire,
That consumed the love that my heart could not tire.

21. Evangelyne S.

I weigh my love
For what is love?
I may not know for now.
But, somehow this love of yours triggered me
Even when I no longer shouldn't, I couldn't.
I may be lost in words but your care and love for me will always be in
my heart
Isn't it crazy that I still think of you
I still feel the warmth of you
Everywhere, I see you
How immature of me to say this
But I just miss your laughter and your way of talking
Oh! if I had the chance to rewind it I would helplessly do so
Oh! if I had the chance to touch you and feel you again I would do so
Because those were the days, I cherished the most.
How could you leave me in this dark and cruel world
Where all I could asked for is YOU
You are the reason that I am happy
You are the reason that I can laugh
You are the reason that I can make my day be filled with butterflies
and love
Do I deserve this
Do I deserve to be left alone here
Do I deserve to not feel your love anymore
I'm sorry

But I miss you dearly

I miss you love

Come back here, come to me

Come and lay on my shoulder like you always did

Like you always talked about everything and made me feel warm.

I can't stay in here without you

I can't love anyone but you

Why did you go and didn't tell me

Why?

It's not easy for me

It's not

No

Oh! my love my heart hurts

I'm bleeding inside

I'm hurt, badly

But who would I talk to about this

With whom I can share this with?

No one.

May your ghost always be with me by my side forever

For that's the only thing that makes me calm and secure

I may be a fool to say this

Yes, I am my love

But I can't I'm sorry

I couldn't stay strong

I would always remember you saying that I should be strong and independent

Yes! I am independent but I can't be strong

I can't be strong not knowing you're not here

I'm crying I'm dying with a deep knife in my heart

I'm stuck in a shallow
In a place that I can't see the light anymore
But as I sit here alone in a dark
I'll always remember you
I'll always love you
Now and forever
And also, in the next life
Cause for now it is goodbye
And for the next I hope it's not
See you my love,
See you in our next life.

22. Jankincy H. L.

Stepping into the burning pyre,
The Melancholic boy plays his final tune.
The cries of many blends into the music,
Some must have said, "He is going too soon!"

One Night, a tune pierced through her senses,
Standing before his hut, Charmed by the melancholic music
Astonished by the Shunned One,
She felt woven with his Soulful playing.

Love lasted for a few melodies from the flute,
The days began to feel drier than the reasons there were to stay.
She began to feel a sting from the return,
The Penalty then shattered the Nickel that started the play.

What trouble did the lovers find,
When Midnight trails were of sweet affairs,
Never expecting the tragic aftermath of the affection
Then the tune began to float on a different air.

The air was humble,
When he reached the call,
She could not act on the deeds that filled her desires then,
So he was bound, by the flute's trails, So he took the fall.

The burning passion of the Lovers appeared
As she throws her shawl aside.
As the Queen leaps to join her lover,
The Flute must have cried.

• 46 •

The Midnight trails of tune that led her there,
Was it their destiny that led them here?
The flute's sharpness then became, then lesser,
And the tune was gone, and so was he.

23. Ehboklang P.

My mother told me to leave quickly,
To help my sister.
It was an odd time, yet, I obeyed.
I walked through rivers and played with the river *ngot*,
Moving mountains and valleys, and racing through sunlight.
Then I found sunny dandelions, I wished on one
And choked on another, in anger, I tore through the rest.
I rushed on, with my mind unease till
I heard the old trees, Oh! sweet thoughtful music they play.
But in disquiet times, I watched them swayed.
Playing cheerless melodies as I passed through.
I, then see my sister weeping and wailing.
Charring sinned bodies, flaming out.
I 'huffed and puffed, I 'huffed and puffed'
For, two souls had crept into the sunless pit.
The souls embraced.
And mother came to take them home.
His flute one hand, his Eve on the other.

24. Glossary

Besli - Bamboo Flute

U Shken - The Preferred Type Of Bamboo For Flute Making

Ha 'per amirphor jingieid, ha tmied kpep ding - in the realm of love, near the furnace glow

U Manik bad Lieng ki shad iphuh – iphieng - Manik and Lieng danced in blossoming love

The Khasi lines above are from a poem *Ka Liengmakaw*, by Jespil syiem depicting Love as deep and everlasting.

The phrase *'per amirphor jingieid* represents a world filled with love a place where passion thrives, untouched by fear or doubt. Their love is all-encompassing, vibrant, and pure.

Thmied-kpep ding symbolizes both the warmth of their passion and the trials they must endure.

Their dance, full of life and energy (*iphuh-iphieng*), marks the beginning of a love that will soon be tested by fate.

Ha jingim, Manik bad Lieng, ki ieid shitrhem - In life Manik and Lieng, Love with all their might

Poh ka Lawarding, ki kdup ki piam shilem - through trials and fire, they embrace on so tight.

Jespil Syiem's final Khasi lines mark the end of *u Manik* and *ka Lieng* journey, which beautifullycaptures their deep love and unwavering commitment.

The phrase *ki ieid shitrhem* signifies passionate love which highlights a love that is profound and lifelong.

The word *Lawarding* represents trials and hardships, while the phrase *ki kdup - ki piam shilem* - expresses their eternal embrace which reflects their deep emotional connection.

Syiem - King